D1232911

# Who Were the Conquistadores?

## History for Kids Series

## Children's Ancient History Books

Left Brain Kids

Educational Books for Children

Conquistadores (conqueror) is the term for leaders of Spanish conquests in America, most specifically in Mexico and Peru.

These conquistadores were considered professional warriors, who used European tactics, cavalry and firearms to win battles.

Their "company" or units underwent prolonged periods of training that were too expensive for non-formal groups. Their armies were composed of Iberian and European soldiers.

Let us get to know some of the most famous conquistadores, who led Spanish expeditions during the 16th century!

Hernan Cortes
led the expedition
to conquer Aztec,
Mexico in 1519.

With about 400 men, he set up his base camp in Veracruz and advanced inland until he secured alliance with Tlaxcala City.

With the help of his allies, he conquered Aztec, the capital city of Tenochtitlan, which is now known as Mexico City.

From 1522 to 1524, he also conquered the Michoacan and Pacific coastal region.

An invasion in Inca, Peru was led by two Spanish adventurers, Diego de Almagro and Francisco Pizarro, who originally came from Panama.

Pizarro left to
conquer Peru
in 1531, along
with one hundred
eighty soldiers
and 37 horses.

He took advantage
of the civil war
that happened
at that time and
captured the ruler
of the Inca natives,
Atahuallpa.

In November 1533, Almagro invaded the Cuzco City, which was the capital of Inca, Peru.

In 1535, Pizarro
founded the new
capital of Lima.

In 1538, a quarrel
among Pizarro and
Almagro erupted
into a civil war,
where Pizarro came
out victorious.

Pizarro was
murdered 3 years
after his victory.

Sebastian de Benalcazar and Gonzalo Jimenez de Quesada led the invasion of Colombia.

In 1541, Pedro de Valdivia explored Chile and founded the City of Santiago.

De Valvidia, de Benalcazar and de Quesada focused more on conquering cities and taking golden treasures instead of governing. Because of this, they were replaced with settlers and administrators from Spain.

Conquering cities in foreign lands would take a lot of strength, power, intellect and wit. These conquistadores have proven their importance in spreading Spain's influence to the world.

Did you enjoy the story of the conquistadores?

Made in the USA
Las Vegas, NV
02 March 2023

68404179R00026